Contents

S0-BFB-594

Living Luther's Catechism

**52 Interactive Devotions on
Luther's Small Catechism
Reproducible for Group Use**

*Written by Michael Awe, Paul Hoyer,
David Loeschen, Douglas Nicely,
Scott Sailer, Steven Sell, John Tape*

Editors: Kenneth Wagener and Rodney Rathmann

This publication is also available in braille and in large print for the visually impaired. Write to the Library for the Blind, 1333 S. Kirkwood Rd., St. Louis, MO 63122-7295; or call 1-800-433-3954.

Quotations from the Small Catechism are from *Luther's Small Catechism with Explanation,* copyright © 1986, 1991 by Concordia Publishing House. All rights reserved.

The quotations from the Lutheran Confessions in this publication are from THE BOOK OF CONCORD: THE CONFESSIONS OF THE EVANGELICAL LUTHERAN CHURCH, edited by Theodore G. Tappert, copyright © 1959 Fortress Press. Used by permission of Augsburg Fortress.

Scripture quotations taken from the HOLY BIBLE: NEW INTERNATIONAL VERSION®. NIV®. Copyright © 1973, 1978, 1984 by International Bible Society. Used by permission of Zondervan Publishing House. All rights reserved.

Scripture quotations marked NKJV are taken from the New King James Version. Copyright © 1979, 1980, 1982 by Thomas Nelson, Inc. Used by permission. All rights reserved.

Copyright © 1998 Concordia Publishing House
3558 South Jefferson Avenue, St. Louis, MO 63118-3968
Manufactured in the United States of America

1   2   3   4   5   6   7   8   9   10   07   06   05   04   03   02   01   00   99   98

Living Luther's Catechism

"I remember that story from Sunday school."

"I memorized that in confirmation."

"I'll never forget an illustration my pastor used a long time ago."

The human mind is a marvelous gift from God. Every day we hear, read, and watch thousands of words and pictures. Our brains process and absorb millions of "bytes" of new information. Some of these images and details stay with us as long as we live. Others are less permanent; we must, then, regularly recall and review what we have learned and understood so that it remains with us.

Living Luther's Catechism is a collection of 52 brief, interactive devotions to help God's people in Christ recall and review the truths of Luther's Small Catechism. For some, the Six Chief Parts are as fresh in our minds today as they were in confirmation instruction. For others, the clear, concise doctrines and explanations are distant memories, waiting to be relearned and applied to new circumstances.

Each devotion in *Living Luther's Catechism* focuses on ways that believers may reflect anew on the fundamentals of the Christian faith and apply God's Word and the Catechism to their daily lives. This discussion-focus approach will remind participants of the oneness we have in Christ as they learn from one another about God's love and care for His people.

The 52 devotions are designed as an introduction or a review for a variety of congregational and personal settings.

Congregational meetings: councils, boards, and committees.

Group meetings: men's and women's groups, older adult groups, youth groups.

Small groups: individuals and couples gathered for study and prayer.

Family and personal use.

Plan for 15–20 minutes of review and discussion. If time permits, encourage further sharing.

It's not necessary to provide Bibles or catechisms for participants. Each devotion has Scripture passages and relevant catechism texts to help the participants appreciate God's truth.

Leaders will want to read the appropriate section in *Luther's Small Catechism with Explanation.*

How to Use These Devotions

Follow these simple steps:

1. Select one of the 52 devotions.
2. Make a sufficient number of copies for your meeting or gathering.
3. Distribute a copy to each participant.
4. For large groups, consider asking participants to form small groups (3–4) to work through the questions. This will give each person an opportunity to share.
5. Read aloud the Scripture and/or Catechism portions.
6. Use the questions provided or raise additional questions in the "For Sharing" section.
7. Use the prayer to conclude the devotion.

Other ideas for use:

- Reproduce and distribute in congregational newsletters.
- Reproduce and distribute in weekly bulletins.
- Reproduce and use for Christian education programs, including confirmation and adult studies.
- Reproduce and make available in your church's narthex for personal and family devotions.

In an age of declining scriptural literacy, doctrinal understanding, and individual and family stewardship, we pray that these devotions will help Christians to celebrate God's grace to us through Jesus our Lord. By the power of the Holy Spirit may we focus again on the rich heritage that is ours as the people of God in Christ.

Luther's Catechism

THE SIX CHIEF PARTS:

"Every morning, and whenever else I have time, I read and recite word for word the Lord's Prayer, the Ten Commandments, the Creed, the Psalms, etc. I must still read and study the Catechism daily, yet I cannot master it as I wish, but must remain a child and pupil of the Catechism, and I do it gladly" (Martin Luther).

If you point these things out to the brothers, you will be a good minister of Christ Jesus, brought up in the truths of the faith and of the good teaching that you have followed. (1 Timothy 4:6)

FOR SHARING

1. "It's not *what* you believe that matters; it's *that* you believe!" In what ways is this statement true of many in today's world?

2. If possible, share a memory from your confirmation instruction. What about your study of the Catechism was meaningful to you?

3. The Catechism, Luther wrote, is a summary and guide to the whole Bible. How do the Six Chief Parts summarize Christian doctrine? How does the Catechism guide us through the teachings of Holy Scripture?

4. Just as Christ is the true focus of the Scriptures, so also Christ is the center of the Catechism. How does each part of the Catechism point to Jesus and His saving work?

5. Why is regular—daily!—devotion time so important for God's people? How can the Catechism be part of your regular devotions?

PRAYER Almighty God, thank You for Your Word of truth. In Your Law You show me my sin, but in the Gospel You bring me forgiveness, life, and salvation in Christ. Strengthen my faith in my Savior every day as I daily study and grow in His Word. In Jesus' name I pray. Amen.

One God

THE FIRST COMMANDMENT

You shall have no other gods. *(Exodus 20:3)*

What does this mean? We should fear, love, and trust in God above all things.

This is what the Lord says—Israel's King and Redeemer, the Lord Almighty: I am the first and I am the last; apart from Me there is no God. (Isaiah 44:6)

FOR SHARING

1. A philosopher once wrote, "Tell me to what you pay attention, and I will tell you who you are." Agree or disagree? Why?

2. The First Commandment, Martin Luther said, is the very first, highest, and best from which all others must proceed. What did he mean? In what ways does the First Commandment "set the tone" for the other commandments?

3. "What is it to have a god?" Luther asks (Large Catechism). "A god is that to which we look for all good and in which we find refuge in every time of need." Describe the gods that people "cling to" in life.

4. Jesus was fully obedient to His Father—obedient to death on a cross (Philippians 2:8). Share how His sacrifice frees us from the demands of the First Commandment.

5. Fear. Love. Trust. What do the words mean for your life as you live in Christ's forgiveness?

PRAYER My Savior God, in Christ I am Your child, and You are my Father. Let me live in Your grace. May Your love permeate every part of my life that I may always desire to reverence You, love You, trust You, and serve You. In Jesus' name I pray. Amen.

God's Name

THE SECOND COMMANDMENT

You shall not misuse the name of the Lord your God. *(Exodus 20:7)*

What does this mean? We should fear and love God so that we do not curse, swear, use satanic arts, lie, or deceive by His name, but call upon it in every trouble, pray, praise, and give thanks.

> **O LORD, our Lord, how majestic is Your name in all the earth! You have set Your glory above the heavens. (Psalm 8:1)**

FOR SHARING

1. "Names are everything," wrote Oscar Wilde. In what ways do names—first, middle, and last names—give us a sense of identity and purpose?

2. How do people misuse God's name today? Why do you think people misuse God's name?

3. From eternity, the name planned for the Messiah was Jesus, Immanuel (Matthew 1:21, 23). What does it mean for you that Jesus was "God with us" at Calvary? What does it mean for your eternal destiny?

4. God's name—Father, Son, and Holy Spirit—was placed on us in Baptism (Matthew 28:19). How does His name shape our identity in the world? How does our Baptism into the triune God strengthen us for daily service?

5. Which name for God best reminds you of His goodness to you today?

PRAYER Gracious God, remind me every day that I am baptized in Your name. Help me to use Your name respectfully and faithfully in all that I say, think, and do. Strengthen me with Your Spirit so that my name as "Christian" will give honor to You. Amen.

God's Word

THE THIRD COMMANDMENT

Remember the Sabbath day by keeping it holy. *(Exodus 20:8)*

What does this mean? We should fear and love God so that we do not despise preaching and His Word, but hold it sacred and gladly hear and learn it.

> **Remember the Sabbath day by keeping it holy. Six days you shall labor and do all your work, but the seventh day is a Sabbath to the Lord your God ... For in six days the Lord made the heavens and the earth, the sea, and all that is in them, but He rested on the seventh day. Therefore the Lord blessed the Sabbath and made it holy. (Exodus 20:8–11)**

FOR SHARING

1. The average church has fewer than 50 percent of its members in worship each week. What kinds of obstacles do you face in attending worship regularly?

2. To keep something holy means "to set it aside for a special, sacred use." What is so special and sacred about weekly worship?

3. The Sabbath is also a day of rest. In what ways is rest vital to your physical life? to your spiritual life?

4. Through faith, the book of Hebrews notes, God's people have a "Sabbath-rest"(4:9). How is Jesus our Sabbath-rest? How does He give you true rest?

5. What does God do for you at every worship service? How do His gifts strengthen you during the week?

PRAYER Jesus, You are Lord of the Sabbath. You are the Lord and Savior of my life. Please forgive me for those times when I was hesitant, reluctant, or negligent about coming to Your Father's house of worship. Thank You for the strength I receive there through Your Word and Sacraments. Help me always to hear Your Word gladly and willingly. In Your name. Amen.

God's Representatives

THE FOURTH COMMANDMENT

Honor your father and your mother. *(Exodus 20:12)*

What does this mean? We should fear and love God so that we do not despise or anger our parents and other authorities, but honor them, serve them, love and cherish them.

Honor your father and your mother, so that you may live long in the land the LORD your God is giving you. (Exodus 20:12)

FOR SHARING

1. A bumper sticker says, *Question Authority.* What "hidden messages" do the words convey? Why is authority a negative concept for many people?

2. Our parents are the first authority figures in our lives. In what ways is the stability and strength of society dependent on the health of the family?

3. What other authority comes from God? How do these authorities reflect God's will for a strong, stable society?

4. Though He possessed all authority in heaven and on earth, Jesus came to earth to obey all true authority. He humbled Himself and submitted to the will of sinful authorities who put Him to death. Share what Jesus' willing sacrifice means to you.

5. Honor, serve, love, and cherish. By the power of God's Spirit, how might we appreciate our parents and other authorities in our life?

PRAYER Lord Jesus, all authority in heaven and on earth has been given to You. Help me to respect those to whom You have chosen as representatives of Your authority: parents, police officers, elected officials, and pastors and leaders who are called by You to serve in Your church. Give those in authority the wisdom they need to make decisions that are pleasing to You and good for Your people. In Jesus' name. Amen.

God's Gift of Life

THE FIFTH COMMANDMENT

You shall not murder. *(Exodus 20:13)*

What does this mean? We should fear and love God so that we do not hurt or harm our neighbor in his body, but help and support him in every physical need.

> **Blessed be Your glorious name, and may it be exalted above all blessing and praise. You alone are the Lord. You made the heavens, even the highest heavens, and all their starry host, the earth and all that is on it, the seas and all that is in them. You give life to everything, and the multitudes of heaven worship You. (Nehemiah 9:5–6)**

FOR SHARING

1. Life is God's gift. How does the creation reveal God's good gift of life?

2. Instead of life, violence and death are often the predominant images—especially in the media! In what ways has violence affected your community? your family? your congregation?

3. It is sinful, Luther notes, to "hurt or harm our neighbor in his body." List specific ways we might hurt and harm others with our words and actions.

4. "The Son of Man," Jesus told His disciples, "will be mocked and flogged and crucified" (Matthew 20:18–19). His death is not, however, random or senseless; it is His sacrifice for the sins of the world. How does Jesus' death bring us life? How does His death take away our fear of death?

5. In what specific ways can we, as God's redeemed children, affirm life in all settings?

PRAYER
Wake us, O Lord, to human need, To go wherever You would lead.
Awake our senses so that we More sensitive to needs may be.

Since you've redeemed us from despair, You've freed us so that we can share;
Our neighbors' problems now we'll bear. Because You love, we love and care.
Amen.

(Joyful Sounds 109).
Text by Phyllis Kersten. Used by permission.

God's Gift of Marriage

THE SIXTH COMMANDMENT

You shall not commit adultery. *(Exodus 20:14)*

What does this mean? We should fear and love God so that we lead a sexually pure and decent life in what we say and do, and husband and wife love and honor each other.

> **Flee from sexual immorality. All other sins a man commits are outside his body, but he who sins sexually sins against his own body. Do you not know that your body is a temple of the Holy Spirit, who is in you, whom you have received from God? You are not your own; you were bought at a price. Therefore honor God with your body. (1 Corinthians 6:18–20)**

FOR SHARING

1. "Sex is like fire. In a fireplace, it's warm and delightful. Outside the hearth, it's destructive and uncontrollable." Explain.

2. Describe, in your own words, a "sexually pure and decent life." Why is it so difficult to live in sexual purity and decency?

3. Jesus' love for sinful human beings led Him to the cross, where He paid the price for our unfaithfulness. What comfort do you have in trusting Him for *full* forgiveness?

4. God created sex! God established marriage and gives His blessing as a man and woman are united as "one flesh" (Genesis 2:24). How can husbands and wives use the gift of sexuality to honor God?

PRAYER Lord, in Your grace You have redeemed every aspect of my life, including my sexuality. Help me to appreciate this gift as a sacred, responsible trust. Please forgive me for those times I have sinned against Your commandment. Direct my life so that I may live to Your glory and praise. In Jesus' name. Amen.

God's Gift of Possessions

THE SEVENTH COMMANDMENT

You shall not steal. *(Exodus 20:15)*

What does this mean? We should fear and love God so that we do not take our neighbor's money or possessions, or get them in any dishonest way, but help him to improve and protect his possessions and income.

> **Therefore each of you must put off falsehood and speak truthfully to his neighbor, for we are all members of one body. ... He who has been stealing must steal no longer, but must work, doing something useful with his own hands, that he may have something to share with those in need. (Ephesians 4:25, 28)**

FOR SHARING

1. Robin Hood. Jesse James. Butch Cassidy and the Sundance Kid. What wrong message do we give by making these individuals into "folk-heroes"?

2. What kinds of actions—both sinful and illegal—come under the category "stealing"? What negative attitudes and behaviors can result from "petty thefts"?

3. A Samaritan in the parable (Luke 10:29–37) gave himself unselfishly for the benefit and welfare of another—a stranger and an enemy! In what ways is Jesus *The* Good Samaritan? How has He rescued and cared for us?

4. Jesus "took" our sins and left them at the cross that we may have new life. How does our new life in Christ affect our attitudes and actions toward others? toward their property and possessions?

5. Share, as time permits, the specific ways you and your congregation can "improve and protect" your neighbor's property.

PRAYER

Heavenly Father, we thank You that You have provided us and our neighbors with material possessions. Help us all to realize that our money and our possessions are gifts from You. Help us to be grateful for all the gifts we have received from Your bountiful goodness. When we are tempted to steal, remind us to look to Your Son, Jesus, for our strength to do Your will. In His name we pray. Amen.

God's Gift of a Good Reputation 9

THE EIGHTH COMMANDMENT

You shall not give false testimony against your neighbor. *(Exodus 20:16).*

What does this mean? We should fear and love God so that we do not tell lies about our neighbor, betray him, slander him, or hurt his reputation, but defend him, speak well of him, and explain everything in the kindest way.

> **Do not let any unwholesome talk come out of your mouths, but only what is helpful for building others up according to their needs, that it may benefit those who listen. And do not grieve the Holy Spirit of God, with whom you were sealed for the day of redemption. (Ephesians 4:29–30)**

FOR SHARING

1. "It is always the best policy to speak the truth, unless of course you are an exceptionally good liar" (Jerome K. Jerome). In what ways does this statement reflect today's standards and practices?

2. Why is reputation so important in business? in relationships?

3. How can lies, betrayal, slander, and gossip destroy lives?

4. In His life and through His death, Jesus was the true and faithful witness to God's plan of salvation. He spoke the truth and demonstrated the truth at the cross. How does the Gospel change us to live in God's truth?

5. What positive results occur when God's forgiven and renewed people "explain everything in the kindest way"?

PRAYER Merciful Father, You created me to be a reflection of Your divine goodness. Yet I have fallen short of Your holy will. I humbly acknowledge my sin and ask Your forgiveness in Christ. Give me Your strength through Your Holy Spirit so that I use Your gift of speech to Your honor and the good of all people. In Jesus' name. Amen.

God's Gift of Contentment

THE NINTH AND TENTH COMMANDMENTS

You shall not covet your neighbor's house. *(Exodus 20:17)*

What does this mean? We should fear and love God so that we do not scheme to get our neighbor's inheritance or house, or get it in a way which only appears right, but help and be of service to him in keeping it.

You shall not covet your neighbor's wife, or his manservant or maidservant, his ox or donkey, or anything that belongs to your neighbor. *(Exodus 20:17)*

What does this mean? We should fear and love God so that we do not entice or force away our neighbor's wife, workers, or animals, or turn them against him, but urge them to stay and do their duty.

> **Keep your lives free from the love of money and be content with what you have, because God has said, "Never will I leave you; never will I forsake you." So we say with confidence, "The Lord is my helper; I will not be afraid. What can man do to me? (Hebrews 13:5–6)**

FOR SHARING

1. "Better a little fire to warm us than a great one to burn us." Explain the saying in the light of our materialistic culture.

2. Describe, in your own words, what it means to *covet*.

3. What sinful desire in the Garden of Eden brought sin into the world? What did Adam and Eve show by their actions?

4. St. Paul writes of Christ Jesus, "Though He was rich, yet for your sakes He became poor, so that you through His poverty might become rich" (2 Corinthians 8:9). How does the Gospel of forgiveness and salvation bring contentment to your life?

5. Share, as time permits, how God's Word is your source of joy, encouragement, and contentment.

PRAYER

Heavenly Father, You have blessed me in ways too numerous to count. Thank You for everything You have given me. Thank You, above all, for salvation in Christ. Strengthen me to live in love toward others so that I may rest content in Your goodness and peace. In Jesus' name. Amen.

The Double-Edged Sword

THE CLOSE OF THE COMMANDMENTS

What does God say of all these commandments? He says: "I, the Lord your God, am a jealous God, punishing the children for the sin of the fathers to the third and fourth generation of those who hate Me, but showing love to a thousand generations of those who love Me and keep My commandments."

What does this mean? God threatens to punish all who break these commandments. Therefore, we should fear His wrath and not do anything against them. But He promises grace and every blessing to all who keep these commandments. Therefore, we should also love and trust in Him and gladly do what He commands.

> **I, the Lord your God, am a jealous God, punishing the children for the sin of the fathers to the third and fourth generation of those who hate Me, but showing love to a thousand generations of those who love Me and keep My commandments. (Exodus 20:5b–6)**

FOR SHARING

1. G. K. Chesterton wrote, "When people cease to believe in God, they don't believe in nothing; they believe in anything." In what ways have his words come true in today's world?

2. The Close of the Commandments reminds us, as Luther notes, that the Law is a "serious matter to God." How do we often trivialize God's commandments by our words and actions?

3. "The Word of God is living and active. Sharper than any double-edged sword" (Hebrews 4:12). Describe how the Bible speaks to us through Law and Gospel.

4. Jesus is the "fulfillment of the Law" (Matthew 5:17–18). How does His perfect obedience and His sacrificial death comfort you in dealing with your temptations and failures?

5. Though we always preach and teach the Law, why is it important that the Gospel of forgiveness, life, and salvation predominate?

PRAYER
God's Word is our great heritage And shall be ours forever;
To spread its light from age to age Shall be our chief endeavor.
Through life it guides our way, In death it is our stay.
Lord, grant, while worlds endure, We keep its teachings pure
Throughout all generations. Amen.

THE APOSTLES' CREED

What is a creed? A creed is a statement of what we believe, teach, and confess.
What is meant by "I believe in God"? It means I trust God and His promises and accept as true all He teaches in the Holy Scriptures.
Why is it called the Apostles' Creed? It is called the Apostles' Creed, not because it was written by the apostles themselves, but because it states briefly the doctrine (teaching) which God gave through the apostles in the Bible. The Creed is trinitarian because the Scriptures reveal God as triune. Christians are baptized in the name of the triune God: Father, Son, and Holy Spirit.

Now faith is being sure of what we hope for and certain of what we do not see. (Hebrews 11:1)

FOR SHARING

1. A World War II bunker near Cologne, France, provided a secret hideout for a small company of soldiers trapped behind enemy lines. As he hid day after day in the darkness, one soldier carved these words on the bunker wall: "I believe in the sun even if I do not see it shining!"
Describe the soldier's faith.

2. "Faith is being sure of what we hope for." How does hope in Christ differ from all other types of hope?

3. To believe in God is to trust His promises. What assurance do Christ's death and resurrection give you that *all* God's promises are true?

4. "Faith is being certain of what we do not see." How does your faith in Christ help you deal with daily trials and troubles?

5. "A Christian is someone who believes the Apostles' Creed." Do you agree or disagree. Why?

PRAYER
Lord, thank You for Your gracious promises in Your Word. Forgive me for the times that I have doubted Your love and grace. Help me to walk by faith at all the different times of my life. In Jesus' name I pray. Amen.

God Our Maker

THE APOSTLES' CREED—THE FIRST ARTICLE

I believe in God the Father Almighty, Maker of heaven and earth.

What does this mean? I believe that God has made me and all creatures; that He has given me my body and soul, eyes, ears, and all my members, my reason and all my senses, and still takes care of them.

> **For you created my inmost being; you knit me together in my mother's womb. I praise You because I am fearfully and wonderfully made; Your works are wonderful, I know that full well. (Psalm 139:13–14)**

FOR SHARING

1. A Bible translator was working on a native dialect. His biggest challenge was to find a word in the language for *believe*. As he was working one day, a young man who had converted to Christianity came into his hut. He had run from a nearby village with a message and was out of breath. Before he could convey the message, he had to sit. As he plopped down into a chair, he said in his language, "Before I give you this message, I need to put all of me into this chair and rest." Suddenly the translator had the word he needed for *believe:* "put all of me into this and rest."
   What kinds of things do people today "put themselves into and rest"?

2. "My soul finds rest in God alone; my salvation comes from Him" (Psalm 62:1). How does God provide our soul with rest?

3. Luther explains that every aspect of life—both physical and spiritual—is God's gift. In what ways does creation bear witness to God's goodness and kindness?

4. St. Paul expressed his confidence, "My God will meet all your needs according to His glorious riches in Christ Jesus" (Philippians 4:19). How does the cross reveal the depth of God's love and care for the world? for you personally?

5. In all of creation, there is no one exactly like you. For what specific qualities and talents are you most thankful?

PRAYER

O Lord, I thank You that You have given me all that I need in this life and have given me the hope of eternal life. Help me to remember that You keep "all of me" in Your care. May I live as one who carries the gracious promises of a loving Creator. In Jesus' name I pray. Amen.

God Our Provider

THE APOSTLES' CREED

I believe in God, the Father Almighty, Maker of heaven and earth.

What does this mean? He also gives me clothing and shoes, food and drink, house and home, wife and children, land, animals, and all I have. He richly and daily provides me with all that I need to support this body and life.

The eyes of all look to You, and You give them their food at the proper time. You open Your hand and satisfy the desires of every living thing. (Psalm 145:15–16)

FOR SHARING

1. What do you consider to be your greatest blessing?

2. The philanthropist Moses Montefiore had as his family motto "Think and Thank." In the old Anglo-Saxon language *thankfulness* means "thinkfulness." In what ways is gratitude tied to remembering?

3. In what ways is God still "richly and daily" providing for His world? In what ways is He always providing you with all that you need?

4. Luther's list of blessings reflects the times and culture in which he lived. What items would be included on your list of blessings from God?

5. Of all of God's good gifts to you, which are you most thankful for today?

PRAYER Lord God, my heart is raised in gratitude for Your bountiful blessings upon our nation's fields, farms, and factories. Even though we are not worthy of Your grace, You provide for all our needs. Help me to be "thinkful" of all Your mercies in Christ. In Jesus' name I pray. Amen.

God Our Defender

THE APOSTLES' CREED—THE FIRST ARTICLE

I believe in God the Father Almighty, Maker of heaven and earth.

What does this mean? He defends me against all danger and guards and protects me from all evil.

> Are not two sparrows sold for a penny? Yet not one of them will fall to the ground apart from the will of your Father. And even the very hairs of your head are all numbered. So don't be afraid; you are worth more than many sparrows. (Matthew 10:29–31)

FOR SHARING

1. Tell about a time when you were in danger or felt overwhelmed by your situation.

2. Danger and evil, Luther reminds us, surround us every day. In addition to the physical dangers, what spiritual dangers do you face?

3. In what ways do we often "let down our guard" against Satan and evil?

4. The Lord Jesus paid the price to defend and save us from the forces of evil and eternal destruction. Explain the role of God the Father in bringing about our salvation.

5. Share how your faith in Christ helps you live and work confidently in His name.

PRAYER
O Lord, You provide care and protection for all Your creation. You give me what I need to stand firm in faith. Thank You for Your love revealed at the cross. Help me to know that I am safe in Your mighty power. In Jesus' name. Amen.

God Our Father

THE APOSTLES' CREED—THE FIRST ARTICLE

I believe in God the Father Almighty, Maker of heaven and earth.

What does this mean? All this He does only out of fatherly, divine goodness and mercy, without any merit or worthiness in me. For all this it is my duty to thank and praise, serve and obey Him. This is most certainly true.

> **For as high as the heavens are above the earth, so great is His love for those who fear Him; as far as the east is from the west, so far has He removed our transgressions from us. As a father has compassion on his children, so the Lord has compassion on those who fear Him. (Psalm 103:11–13)**

FOR SHARING

1. A guest at a reception told President Lincoln that people were saying the welfare of the nation depended on God and Abraham Lincoln.
   Lincoln replied, "They are half right."
   In what ways do people rely on human ability in difficult circumstances?

2. *"All this,"* Luther notes, God does out of "fatherly, divine goodness and mercy, without any merit or worthiness in me." How do his words exclude all boasting?

3. Share an example of a benevolent father.

4. We are precious to God, not because of what we are, but because of who God is—the Savior God in Christ. Describe the perfect fatherhood of God.

5. How is witnessing to God's love in Christ a response of thanks and praise?

PRAYER
Heavenly Father, thank You for Your goodness and mercy, freely given to me in the Lord Jesus. Help me that I may serve You with a grateful and obedient heart. In Jesus' name. Amen.

Incarnate Lord

THE APOSTLES' CREED—THE SECOND ARTICLE

I believe in Jesus Christ, His only Son, our Lord, who was conceived by the Holy Spirit, born of the Virgin Mary.

What does this mean? I believe that Jesus Christ, true God, begotten of the Father from eternity, and also true man, born of the Virgin Mary, is my Lord.

> **She will give birth to a Son, and you are to give Him the name Jesus, because He will save His people from their sins. (Matthew 1:21)**

FOR SHARING

1. Share your most cherished Christmas memory. What makes Christmas special in your home or family?

2. "The coming of Jesus into the world is the most stupendous event in human history" (Malcolm Muggeridge).
   "Filling the world he lies in a manger" (St. Augustine).
   "Because eternity was closeted in time, he is my open door to forever" (Luci Shaw).
   Describe, in your own words, the wonder and glory of the incarnation.

3. Thomas confessed of Jesus, "My Lord and my God!" (John 20:28). What does the divinity of Christ mean for your daily life?

4. Jesus is also true man. What does it mean to you that Jesus is fully and completely human—yet without sin?

5. The name Jesus ("the Lord saves") and Christ ("the Anointed") shows us a glimpse of God's relationship to us. What has Jesus Christ saved you from? What has he saved you for?

PRAYER My Lord Jesus, thank You for being true God and true man. Thank You for saving me from sin, death, and the devil. Give me Your encouragement to confess You to my family, friends, and neighbors. Help me to serve You by serving others. In Your name I pray. Amen.

Crucified Lord

THE APOSTLES' CREED—THE SECOND ARTICLE

I believe in Jesus Christ, … who … suffered under Pontius Pilate, was crucified, died and was buried.

What does this mean? [He] has redeemed me, a lost and condemned person, purchased and won me from all sins, from death and from the power of the devil; not with gold or silver, but with His holy, precious blood and with His innocent suffering and death.

For you know that it was not with perishable things such as silver or gold that you were redeemed from the empty way of life handed down to you from your forefathers, but with the precious blood of Christ, a lamb without blemish or defect. (1 Peter 1:18–19)

FOR SHARING

1. A "lost and condemned" person has little hope in life. What situations in our world today seem to have no hope? In what ways do people today live "condemned"?

2. Describe the shame of crucifixion.

3. *To redeem* means "to buy back." By His death Jesus bought us back from slavery. How were we enslaved? How do St. Peter's words "the empty way of life" apply to human life without Christ?

4. Jesus' sacrifice was *priceless.* What does His death reveal about God's love for the world? for you?

5. Instead of an "empty life," we have "full life" in Christ (John 10:10). Share, if possible, a blessing from God that has brought you joy and contentment.

PRAYER Lord Jesus, my Savior and Friend, I thank You for walking the way of the cross for me, You are my treasure in life. Give me Your strength, that I may rest assured in Your salvation. Give me new hope every day that I may share Your love with others. In Your name I pray. Amen.

Risen Lord

THE APOSTLES' CREED—THE SECOND ARTICLE

I believe in Jesus Christ, ... He descended into hell. The third day He rose again from the dead.

What does this mean? That I may be His own and live under Him in His kingdom and serve Him in everlasting righteousness, innocence, and blessedness.

"Where, O death, is your victory? Where, O death, is your sting?" The sting of death is sin, and the power of sin is the law. But thanks be to God! He gives us the victory through our Lord Jesus Christ. (1 Corinthians 15:55–57)

FOR SHARING

1. What was the most exciting victory you have witnessed?

2. Jesus' descent into hell was an announcement of His victory over sin, death, and Satan. In what ways did He defeat each of these enemies?

3. Without the resurrection of Christ from the dead, St. Paul writes, "Your faith is futile; you are still in your sins" (1 Corinthians 15:17). Explain Paul's words.

4. Tell about the righteousness, innocence, and blessedness Christ has brought to your life.

5. Tell of a time when Christ's victory over death was especially meaningful for you.

PRAYER Lord Jesus, thank You for the victory You won over sin, death, and Satan. You have called me to be Your child in my Baptism. Help me to see Your death and resurrection as my anchor in life. Give me Your strength that I might live as Your new creation. In Your name I pray. Amen.

Exalted Lord

THE APOSTLES' CREED—THE SECOND ARTICLE

I believe in Jesus Christ, ... He ascended into heaven and sits at the right hand of God, the Father Almighty. From thence He will come to judge the living and the dead.

What does this mean? Just as He is risen from the dead, lives and reigns to all eternity. This is most certainly true.

> **Since, then, you have been raised with Christ, set your hearts on things above, where Christ is seated at the right hand of God. Set your minds on things above, not on earthly things. For you died, and your life is now hidden with Christ in God. (Colossians 3: 1–3)**

FOR SHARING

1. Who, in your opinion, are the greatest rulers in human history? What made them great?

2. Jesus rules His church. How does Jesus rule and govern His church?

3. Before His ascension to heaven, Jesus gave His disciples a commission: "You will be My witnesses" (Acts 1:8). What is the church's witness to the world? In what ways are we encouraged to know that Jesus lives and empowers our witness?

4. Jesus will return again to "judge the living and the dead." Describe what will happen on Judgment Day.

5. Are you looking forward to the judgment? Why or why not?

PRAYER

Lord Jesus, exalted Savior, be with me until You come to take me home to be with You. Prepare my heart that I may be always ready to meet You. Strengthen me to live in harmony with family, friends, and all other people. Make me your faithful witness to those who do not yet know You as their Savior. Let me firmly believe Your promise that You will give me life eternal. In Your name I pray. Amen.

Lord and Giver of Life

THE APOSTLES' CREED—THE THIRD ARTICLE

I believe in the Holy Spirit, …

What does this mean? I believe that I cannot by my own reason or strength believe in Jesus Christ, my Lord, or come to Him; but the Holy Spirit has called me by the Gospel, enlightened me with His gifts, sanctified and kept me in the true faith.

No one can say, "Jesus is Lord," except by the Holy Spirit. (1 Corinthians 12:3)

FOR SHARING

1. "The fool says in his heart, 'There is no God' " (Psalm 14:1). What reasons do people give for *not* believing in God?

2. "You were dead in your transgressions and sins" (Ephesians 2:1). What do St. Paul's words convey about the human condition apart from Christ? What evidence do you see of "spiritual death" in the world?

3. The Holy Spirit, Luther notes, *calls* and *enlightens* people by the Gospel. What comfort do you have in knowing your salvation and conversion are God's work from start to finish?

4. The Holy Spirit, Jesus promised, "will testify about Me" (John 15:26). What has the Spirit brought you to know and believe about Jesus and His plan for your life?

5. The Holy Spirit is not a one-time gift from God, but rather a gift that keeps on giving: He sanctifies and keeps us in the true faith. Tell about the work of the Spirit in your life today.

PRAYER Come, Holy Spirit, fill the hearts of the faithful,
and kindle in them the fire of Your love.
Thank You for calling me to Christ by the Gospel. Keep me in the salvation my Lord has given to me. Bless me with Your presence and grant me a deep trust in my Savior day by day. Help me to share this gift of faith with all people. In Jesus' name. Amen.

Community of Saints

THE APOSTLES' CREED—THE THIRD ARTICLE

I believe in ... the holy Christian church, the communion of saints.

What does this mean? In the same way He calls, gathers, enlightens, and sanctifies the whole Christian church on earth, and keeps it with Jesus Christ in the one true faith.

To all in Rome who are loved by God and called to be saints: Grace and peace to you from God our Father and from the Lord Jesus Christ. (Romans 1:7)

FOR SHARING

1. "She's a saint!" From the world's perspective, what makes a person a saint? In what ways does "saint" have a negative connotation today?

2. The church is the communion of saints—people set apart by God in Christ through the Gospel. In what sense is the church an "invisible community"? A "visible community"?

3. We are, Luther notes, "at the same time saint and sinner." How are we a saint? In what way are we still a sinner?

4. Sainthood is a pure gift from God made possible only through Jesus' life, death, and resurrection. What difference has the gift of forgiveness and salvation in Christ made in your life?

5. "Be alert," St. Paul writes, "and always keep on praying for all the saints" (Ephesians 6:18). What specifically can you pray for God's church—His saints—today?

PRAYER Heavenly Father, I thank You that You have made me a saint through Your Son, Jesus Christ, my Lord. I ask that You continue to bless me with Your Spirit so that I might lead a life worthy of Your calling. Encourage me to share this gift of sainthood with my friends, relatives, and all other people that I meet. In Jesus' name. Amen.

True Treasure

THE APOSTLES' CREED—THE THIRD ARTICLE

I believe in … the forgiveness of sins.

What does this mean? In this Christian church He daily and richly forgives all my sins and the sins of all believers.

He is the atoning sacrifice for our sins, and not only for ours but also for the sins of the whole world. (1 John 2:2)

FOR SHARING

1. A Spanish poet wrote, "If I die, I forgive you; if I recover, we shall see." Is this forgiveness? Explain.

2. In worship we confess to God, "We have sinned against You in thought, word, and deed, by what we have done and by what we have left undone." What do these words tell us about sin and its influence in our lives?

3. A friend confides, "God could never forgive me for what I've done. I'm beyond redemption." How would you respond?

4. Luther wrote in his 95 Theses, "The treasure of the church is the Holy Gospel of the glory and grace of God" (62). Why is the Gospel our one, true treasure in life?

5. In what ways does Christ's "daily and rich" forgiveness enable you to live in an *unforgiving* world?

PRAYER Heavenly Father, thank You that You have forgiven all my sins in the name of Jesus, my Redeemer. Give me courage and the resolve to forgive others who sin against me. Help me to share forgiveness in every relationship. I thank and praise You for my new life and ask that You guide me to greater love and compassion toward all people. In Jesus' name. Amen.

THE APOSTLES' CREED—THE THIRD ARTICLE

I believe in ... the resurrection of the body, and the life everlasting. Amen.

What does this mean? On the Last Day He will raise me and all the dead, and give eternal life to me and all believers in Christ.

> **We believe that Jesus died and rose again and so we believe that God will bring with Jesus those who have fallen asleep in Him. (1 Thessalonians 4:14)**

FOR SHARING

1. What false ideas about life after death are common in our day?

2. Eternal life, Jesus assures us, is ours from the moment we believe in Him (John 5:24). Yet we still live in a sinful world and carry around our sinful nature. As you trust and live for Christ, what challenges and obstacles do you experience?

3. To what do you most look forward when you think about the "Last Day"?

4. Jesus' resurrection assures us that we will be raised to life when He returns in glory. In what ways does His victory over sin, death, and Satan give you hope for the future? for eternity?

5. God gives eternal life in Christ to all who believe and are baptized. How can you celebrate eternal life *now?*

PRAYER Dear Father in heaven, I thank You that You have chosen me to be Your child. Bless me with the ability to properly use the wonderful gift of eternal life. Help me to trust in Your promise of salvation through Christ. Encourage me to share this precious gift with family, friends, and everyone I meet. Help me to appreciate this gift and to look forward to the Last Day when I shall fully enjoy eternal life with You, my Father. Amen.

The Good Father

THE LORD'S PRAYER—INTRODUCTION

Our Father who art in heaven.

What does this mean? With these words God tenderly invites us to believe that He is our true Father and that we are His true children, so that with all boldness and confidence we may ask Him as dear children ask their dear father.

> **For you did not receive a spirit that makes you a slave again to fear, but you received the Spirit of sonship. And by Him we cry, "Abba, Father." The Spirit Himself testifies with our spirit that we are God's children. (Romans 8:15–16)**

FOR SHARING

1. Share a good memory about your father or a father figure in your life.

2. What sort of Father do you think about when you pray the words "Our Father"? How would you describe God as *Father*?

3. In what ways have we, as God's children, disappointed our Father in our family life and relationships?

4. We are family because the Father's one and only Son has paid the price for our redemption. What does it mean to live as brothers and sisters in Christ?

5. In Christ we can pray with "all boldness and confidence." Share how Christ's love and forgiveness encourage you to approach God in daily prayer.

PRAYER

[Abba,] Father, who from heav'n above Has told us here to live in love
And with our fellow Christians share Our mutual burdens and our prayer,
Teach us no thoughtless word to say But from our inmost heart to pray.

THE LORD'S PRAYER—THE FIRST PETITION

Hallowed be Thy name.

What does this mean? God's name is certainly holy in itself, but we pray in this petition that it may be kept holy among us also.

How is God's name kept holy? God's name is kept holy when the Word of God is taught in its truth and purity, and we, as the children of God, also lead holy lives according to it. Help us to do this, dear Father in heaven! But anyone who teaches or lives contrary to God's Word profanes the name of God among us. Protect us from this, heavenly Father!

Praise the Lord, O my soul; all my inmost being, praise His holy name. (Psalm 103:1)

FOR SHARING

1. In what ways do people profane God's name?

2. God—and His name—are holy. We are sinful—unholy. How do we bring dishonor and disgrace to His holy name?

3. Describe how Jesus' sacrifice makes us "holy and blameless" in God's sight (Ephesians 1:4).

4. In what specific ways do God's people, by the power of the Holy Spirit, keep God's name holy?

PRAYER
[Father,] Your name be hallowed. Help us, Lord,
In purity to keep Your Word
That to the glory of Your name
We walk before You free from blame.
Let no false teaching us pervert;
All poor deluded souls convert.

© 1998 CPH   Scripture quotations NIV® by permission of Zondervan.

Of Power, Grace, and Glory

THE LORD'S PRAYER—THE SECOND PETITION

Thy kingdom come.

What does this mean? The kingdom of God certainly comes by itself without our prayer, but we pray in this petition that it may come to us also.

How does God's kingdom come? God's kingdom comes when our heavenly Father gives us His Holy Spirit, so that by His grace we believe His holy Word and lead godly lives here in time and there in eternity.

> **The time has come," He said. "The kingdom of God is near. Repent and believe the good news! (Mark 1:15)**

FOR SHARING

1. What comes to mind when you hear the phrase "kingdom of God"? What positive and negative connotations does the word *kingdom* have today?

2. Throughout history, subjects have often rebelled or revolted against kings and kingdoms. In what ways do we rebel against the King of the universe?

3. Jesus' public preaching ministry began with the call to repent and believe the Good News (Mark 1:15). How are these words summarize His work? How do His words apply to you every day?

4. St. Paul writes, God "has rescued us from the dominion of darkness and brought us into the kingdom of the Son He loves, in whom we have redemption, the forgiveness of sins" (Colossians 1:13). How has the Spirit brought you into God's kingdom? How does the Spirit keep you in the kingdom?

5. God rules over the whole universe (the Kingdom of Power), over the church on earth (the Kingdom of Grace), and over the church and angels in heaven (the Kingdom of Glory). How does God's rule in all three kingdoms give you comfort and hope today?

PRAYER [Father,] Your kingdom come. Guard Your domain And Your eternal righteous reign. The Holy [Spirit] enrich our day With gifts attendant on our way. Break Satan's pow'r, defeat his rage; Preserve Your Church from age to age.

Copyright © 1980 Concordia Publishing House. All rights reserved.

© 1998 CPH Scripture quotations NIV® by permission of Zondervan.

His Good and Gracious Will

THE LORD'S PRAYER—THE THIRD PETITION

Thy will be done on earth as it is in heaven.

What does this mean? The good and gracious will of God is done even without our prayer, but we pray in this petition that it may be done among us also.
How is God's will done? God's will is done when He breaks and hinders every evil plan and purpose of the devil, the world, and our sinful nature, which do not want us to hallow God's name or let His kingdom come; and when He strengthens and keeps us firm in His Word and faith until we die. This is His good and gracious will.

> **[Jesus said,] "And this is the will of Him who sent Me, that I shall lose none of all that He has given Me, but raise them up at the last day." (John 6:39)**

FOR SHARING

1. "Where is God leading me?" Share, if possible, a specific time when this question weighed heavily on your heart and mind.

2. "Thy will be done." Often, however, our inward prayer is "My will be done." Why do our prayers often become "self-centered" rather than "God-centered"?

3. How do the devil and the world work to undermine God's will? How does our sinful nature resist God's will?

4. The Father's will is eternal life for all who believe in Jesus (John 6:39). How did Jesus win eternal life for us? In what ways does the Gospel triumph over "every evil plan" that we face in life?

5. Share how God, through Law and Gospel in the Scriptures, gives you knowledge and understanding of His will in Christ.

PRAYER [Father,] Your gracious will on earth be done As it is done before Your throne,
That patiently we may obey In good or bad times all You say.
Curb flesh and blood and ev'ry ill That sets itself against Your will.

© 1998 CPH   Scripture quotations NIV® by permission of Zondervan.

Daily Bread

THE LORD'S PRAYER—THE FOURTH PETITION

Give us this day our daily bread.

What does this mean? God certainly gives daily bread to everyone without our prayers, even to all evil people, but we pray in this petition that God would lead us to realize this and to receive our daily bread with thanksgiving.

What is meant by daily bread? Daily bread includes everything that has to do with the support and needs of the body, such as food, drink, clothing, shoes, house, home, land, animals, money, goods, a devout husband or wife, devout children, devout workers, devout and faithful rulers, good government, good weather, peace, health, self-control, good reputation, good friends, faithful neighbors, and the like.

The eyes of all look to You, and You give them their food at the proper time. You open Your hand and satisfy the desires of every living thing. (Psalm 145:15–16)

FOR SHARING

1. Daily bread is everything we need for a healthy, stable life. What specific blessings in Luther's list do you most appreciate in your life? What additional blessings might you include?

2. Though God promised to provide daily manna for His people in the desert, they gathered more than a daily ration (Exodus 16). In what ways are we tempted to ask for *more* than our daily bread? What may be the result?

3. Luther reminds us, "God certainly gives daily bread to everyone without our prayers, even to all evil people." What evidence do you see that God extends His kindness to all people, without any "merit or worthiness" in them?

4. Jesus is the "bread of life" (John 6:35). How does His death and resurrection provide for our ultimate daily and eternal needs?

5. Share a time when you were grateful for God's gift of "daily bread"

PRAYER [Father,] give us this day our daily bread And let us all be clothed and fed.
From warfare, rioting, and strife, Disease, and famine save our life
That we in honest peace may live, To care and greed no entrance give.

© 1998 CPH   Scripture quotations NIV® by permission of Zondervan.

Forgiven to Forgive

THE LORD'S PRAYER—THE FIFTH PETITION

And forgive us our trespasses as we forgive those who trespass against us.

What does this mean? We pray in this petition that our Father in heaven would not look at our sins, or deny our prayer because of them. We are neither worthy of the things for which we pray, nor have we deserved them, but we ask that He would give them all to us by grace, for we daily sin much and surely deserve nothing but punishment. So we too will sincerely forgive and gladly do good to those who sin against us.

If anyone says, "I love God," yet hates his brother, he is a liar. For anyone who does not love his brother, whom he has seen, cannot love God, whom he has not seen. And He has given us this command: Whoever loves God must also love his brother. (1 John 4: 20–21)

FOR SHARING

1. "I don't get mad; I get even." When have you been tempted to respond in this way?

2. In what ways does the refusal to forgive affect family and social structures?

3. "We daily sin much and surely deserve nothing but punishment," Luther writes. What struggles do you face daily because of the "Old Adam" in you?

4. Jesus' prayer from the cross was, "Father, forgive them, for they do not know what they are doing" (Luke 23:34). Describe the full forgiveness that Christ won and gives to us at Calvary.

5. "Bear with each other and forgive whatever grievances you may have against one another. Forgive as the Lord forgave you" (Colossians 3:13). Motivated by Christ and His mercy and love, how do we "bear with each other" and live under His cross?

PRAYER
[Father,] forgive our sins, let grace outpour That they may trouble us no more;
We too will gladly those forgive Who harm us by the way they live.
Help us in each community To serve with love and unity.

Copyright © Concordia Publishing House. All rights reserved.

© 1998 CPH   Scripture quotations NIV® by permission of Zondervan.

Temptation

THE LORD'S PRAYER—THE SIXTH PETITION

And lead us not into temptation.

What does this mean? God tempts no one. We pray in this petition that God would guard and keep us so that the devil, the world, and our sinful nature may not deceive us or mislead us into false belief, despair, or other great shame and vice. Although we are attacked by these things, we pray that we may finally overcome them and win the victory.

No temptation has seized you except what is common to man. And God is faithful; He will not let you be tempted beyond what you can bear. But when you are tempted, He will also provide a way out so that you can stand up under it. (1 Corinthians 10:13)

FOR SHARING

1. Temptation! The word brings to mind our human weakness and limitations. List common temptations in our world today.

2. Luther reminds us that the unholy trinity—the devil, the world, and our own sinful nature—often lead us into false belief, despair, and other great shame and vice. He also commented, "You can't keep the birds from flying overhead, but you can keep them from building a nest in your hair." Explain.

3. St. Paul writes that God will "provide a way out so that you can stand up" under temptation (1 Corinthians 10:13). How has God strengthened you to stand up to temptation? What "exits" has He provided?

4. Jesus faced temptation, was obedient to His heavenly Father, and defeated the devil (Matthew 4). Later, He showed His complete, perfect obedience in suffering and dying for our sins. In what ways can Jesus' sacrificial obedience help us when we are tempted?

5. In what ways can Christians help and support one another in times of temptation?

PRAYER Lead not into temptation, Lord, Where our grim foe and all his horde
Would vex our souls on ev'ry hand. Help us resist, help us to stand
Firm in the faith, armed with Your might; Your Spirit gives Your children light.

© 1998 CPH   Scripture quotations NIV® by permission of Zondervan.

THE LORD'S PRAYER—THE SEVENTH PETITION

But deliver us from evil.

What does this mean? We pray in this petition, in summary, that our Father in heaven would rescue us from every evil of body and soul, possessions and reputation, and finally, when our last hour comes, give us a blessed end, and graciously take us from this valley of sorrow to Himself in heaven.

> **Put on the full armor of God so that you can take your stand against the devil's schemes. For our struggle is not against flesh and blood, but against the rulers, against the authorities, against the powers of this dark world and against the spiritual forces of evil in the heavenly realms. Therefore put on the full armor of God, so that when the day of evil comes, you may be able to stand your ground, and after you have done everything, to stand. (Ephesians 6:11–13)**

FOR SHARING

1. Share an example of how evil has affected our world or your life.

2. "Once we assuage our conscience by calling something a 'necessary evil,' it begins to look more and more necessary and less and less evil." Agree or disagree? In what ways do we try to justify our sinful choices and actions?

3. The Lord Jesus "gave Himself to rescue us from the present evil age, according to the will of our God and Father" (Galatians 1:4). How did He defeat Satan? What does His victory mean for you?

4. How can we daily "put on the full armor of God" to resist evil in our world?

5. "I'm but a stranger here, heav'n is my home." Reflect on the joy of heaven, where in Christ all believers will experience full and final rescue from all evil.

PRAYER Deliver us from evil days, From ev'ry dark and trying maze;
Redeem us from eternal death, Console us when we yield our breath.
Give us at last a blessed end; Receive our souls, O faithful friend.

It Shall Be So

THE LORD'S PRAYER—CONCLUSION

For Thine is the kingdom and the power and the glory forever and ever. Amen.

What does this mean? This means that I should be certain that these petitions are pleasing to our Father in heaven, and are heard by Him; for He Himself has commanded us to pray in this way and has promised to hear us. Amen, amen, which means "yes, yes, it shall be so."

> For no matter how many promises God has made, they are "Yes" in Christ. And so through Him the "Amen" is spoken by us to the glory of God. (2 Corinthians 1:20)

FOR SHARING

1. A pastor prayed for rain during the Sunday morning service. After lunch, his family prepared to go out for the afternoon. "Here's the umbrella, daddy," the four-year old daughter said.
   "Why do we need an umbrella?" the pastor asked the child.
   "We prayed for rain this morning," she replied. "Don't you expect God to answer our prayers?"
   Tell about a time when you were surprised by God's answer to your prayer. *What were you expecting?*

2. When is praying difficult for you? When is praying a great comfort and joy?

3. A Christian woman remarked, "God has two answers to our prayers: *Yes,* and *Something Better!*" Explain.

4. In Christ, God speaks His Yes! to all of His promises (2 Corinthians 1:20). What assurance of God's love and care does Christ's sacrifice give you?

5. What can you pray for your congregation *today?*

PRAYER Amen, that is, it shall be so. Make our faith strong that we may know
We need not doubt but shall receive All that we ask, as we believe.
On Your great promise we lay claim. Our faith says amen in Your name.

Sacred Gifts

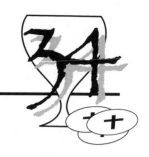

THE SACRAMENTS

What is a Sacrament?
A sacrament is a sacred act
A. instituted by God,
B. in which God Himself has joined His Word of promise to a visible element,
C. and by which He offers, gives, and seals the forgiveness of sins earned by Christ.

[God] chose the lowly things of this world and the despised things—and the things that are not—to nullify the things that are. (1 Corinthians 1:28)

FOR SHARING

1. Exasperated, a man walked into his pastor's office. "Pastor, nothing is holy or sacred any more." Agree or disagree? Explain your answer.

2. God delivers extraordinary gifts in ordinary packages. He gives His forgiveness, life, and salvation through words, water, bread and wine. How does this truth illustrate St. Paul's words? (1 Corinthians 1:28).

3. Together with the Word, the sacraments—Baptism and the Lord's Supper—are the "Means of Grace." God works in our lives through these chosen means. Explain.

4. The sacraments are "visible Gospel." Why do you suppose God gives us—and bless us with—a visible Gospel?

5. At what times in your life have the sacraments been especially important to you?

PRAYER O Lord Jesus, thank You for the sacraments through which You offer, give, and seal the forgiveness of my sins. Remind me every day of my Baptism into Your death and resurrection. Give me joy every time I receive Your body and blood in Your holy Supper. Let me live each day in Your grace and power. In Your holy name I pray. Amen.

God's Promise in Baptism

THE SACRAMENT OF HOLY BAPTISM

What is Baptism?
Baptism is not just plain water, but it is the water included in God's command and combined with God's word.

> **Therefore go and make disciples of all nations, baptizing them in the name of the Father and of the Son and of the Holy Spirit. (Matthew 28:19)**

FOR SHARING

1. Ben Franklin wrote in *Poor Richard's Almanac,* "When the well's dry, we know the worth of water." When have you most appreciated water?

2. Tell about a memorable Baptism in your family or congregation.

3. Martin Luther wrote, "You must esteem Baptism as something high, glorious, and excellent. … If you look upon Baptism as being only water, then you will consider it to be a paltry and ordinary thing" (LW 51.183). Why is it difficult to believe that God gives great blessings through water and His Word?

4. How does Baptism connect you with the Lord and His death and resurrection? How does Baptism connect you with others?

5. "The church is a baptizing community." How does this truth shape your congregation's attitude toward and mission to your community?

PRAYER Heavenly Father, thank You for sending me Your Holy Spirit through my Baptism. Help me to live Your amazing grace in my life so that others may see You in and through me. In Jesus' name I pray. Amen.

God's Blessings in Baptism

THE SACRAMENT OF HOLY BAPTISM

What benefits does Baptism give?
It works forgiveness of sins, rescues from death and the devil, and gives
eternal salvation to all who believe this, as the words and promises of God declare.

Whoever believes and is baptized will be saved, but whoever does not believe will be condemned. (Mark 16:16)

FOR SHARING

1. Most jobs include salary or wage *and benefits*? In what ways are these benefits vital to our daily welfare?

2. What, according to Martin Luther's explanation, are Baptism's benefits? How does each benefit apply to your daily life?

3. Baptism saves. But what condemns? Give an example of how a person can be a Christian and not be baptized.

4. At His baptism, Jesus publicly identified Himself with sinful human beings and revealed Himself as our substitute (Matthew 3:13–17). How does Your Baptism identify you with Christ? In what ways is He your substitute?

5. How can the daily remembrance of your Baptism bring you joy and comfort in life?

PRAYER

Heavenly Father, I praise You for the many benefits that You have given to me through my Baptism. I especially thank You for the forgiveness of all my sins, life, and salvation. By the power of Your Holy Spirit, keep me ever mindful of Your rich blessings through water and the Word. In Jesus' name. Amen.

God's Power in Baptism

THE SACRAMENT OF HOLY BAPTISM

How can water do such great things?
Certainly not just water, but the word of God in and with the water
does these things, along with the faith which trusts this word of God in the water. For without God's word the water is plain water and no Baptism. But with the word of God it is a Baptism, that is, a life-giving water, rich in grace, and a washing of the new birth in the Holy Spirit, as St. Paul says in Titus, chapter three:

He saved us through the washing of rebirth and renewal by the Holy Spirit, whom He poured out on us generously through Jesus Christ our Savior, so that, having been justified by His grace, we might become heirs having the hope of eternal life. This is a trustworthy saying. (Titus 3:5–8)

FOR SHARING

1. What demonstrations of awesome power have you witnessed in your life?

2. Connected to the Word of God, the water of Baptism is "life-giving," "rich in grace," and "a washing of the new birth."

   Baptism is *life-giving.* We are by nature _____

   Baptism is *rich in grace.* We are by nature _____

   Baptism is a *washing of the new birth.* We are by nature _____

3. "When the devil sees Baptism and hears the word sounding, to him it is like a bright sun and he will not stay there" (Martin Luther). In what ways is Baptism like the splendor and power of the sun?

4. "God's words of institution put these blessings [forgiveness, life, and salvation] into Baptism. Faith, which trusts this word of God in the water, takes the blessings out and makes them our own" (*Luther's Small Catechism with Explanation*, Q 253). Explain.

5. The power of Baptism is the power of the Gospel—the Holy Spirit's gift of forgiveness, life, and salvation to all who believe (Romans 1:16–17). How is the Gospel working powerfully in your life? in your congregation?

PRAYER O Lord God, thank You for Your powerful Holy Spirit. I praise You for the many blessings You give to me daily through my Baptism. Continue to renew and strengthen me by Your amazing grace. In Jesus' name. Amen.

God's New Life in Baptism

THE SACRAMENT OF HOLY BAPTISM

What does such baptizing with water indicate?
It indicates that the Old Adam in us should by daily contrition and repentance be drowned and die with all sins and evil desires, and that a new man should daily emerge and arise to live before God in righteousness and purity forever.

We were therefore buried with Him through baptism into death in order that, just as Christ was raised from the dead through the glory of the Father, we too may live a new life. (Romans 6:4)

FOR SHARING

1. "A good beginning makes a good ending." Apply this proverb to daily life.

2. How do we know that the "Old Adam" still lives in us?

3. Jesus was "delivered over to death for our sins and raised to life for our justification" (Romans 4:25). What does His sacrifice mean for you every day? How does His victory encourage you in your work?

4. "A Christian life is nothing else than a daily Baptism, once begun and ever continued" (Large Catechism). Explain.

5. In what specific ways can you share Christ's new life in you with others?

PRAYER O God, Father, Son, and Holy Spirit, thank You for washing me and making me Your child through my Baptism. Continue to renew, cleanse, and restore me to Yourself through Your Word and Sacraments. In Jesus' name. Amen.

Confess and Receive

CONFESSION

What is Confession? Confession has two parts.
First that we confess our sins, and second, that we receive absolution, that is, forgiveness, from the pastor as from God Himself, not doubting, but firmly believing that by it our sins are forgiven before God in heaven.

> **If we claim to be without sin, we deceive ourselves and the truth is not in us. If we confess our sins, [God] is faithful and just and will forgive us our sins and purify us from all unrighteousness. (1 John 1:8–9)**

FOR SHARING

1. During a summit meeting between Khrushchev and Kennedy, the president said to the Russian premier, "Do you ever admit to a mistake?"
   "Certainly I do," Khrushchev replied. "In a recent speech I admitted all of Stalin's mistakes."
   Why is it difficult for many people to say, "I made a mistake"?

2. To *confess* means to agree with and say back to God what He has first spoken to us. What does God's Law tell us about ourselves?

3. Luther wrote, "When I urge you to go to confession, I am simply urging you to be a Christian." Explain.

4. Jesus is the "faithful and just" Savior who forgives us and purifies us from all unrighteousness. How does Jesus provide these gifts to you personally?

5. The pastor's announcement of forgiveness is the announcement of *God's* forgiveness. Why is it important to know that *Christ* speaks His Word in the absolution?

PRAYER
Gracious Father, I know what a sinner I am. But I also know what a loving God You are. Thank you for giving Your Son to death for me and all people. Create in me a clean heart, and lead me to live as Your child, guided by Your Word and Spirit. In Jesus' name. Amen.

Comfort for Troubled Hearts

CONFESSION

What sins should we confess?
Before God we should plead guilty of all sins, even those we are not aware of, as we do in the Lord's Prayer; but before the pastor we should confess only those sins which we know and feel in our hearts.
Which are these?
Consider your place in life according to the Ten Commandments: Are you a father, mother, son, daughter, husband, wife, or worker? Have you been disobedient, unfaithful, or lazy? Have you been hot-tempered, rude, or quarrelsome? Have you hurt someone by your words or deeds? Have you stolen, been negligent, wasted anything, or done any harm?

> When I kept silent, my bones wasted away through my groaning all day long.
>
> For day and night Your hand was heavy upon me; my strength was sapped as in the heat of summer.
>
> Then I acknowledged my sin to You and did not cover up my iniquity. I said, "I will confess my transgressions to the Lord"—and You forgave the guilt of my sins. (Psalm 32:3–5)

FOR SHARING

1. "Confession is good for the soul." Share a story or an example that demonstrates the truth of this adage.

2. The sins "we know and feel in our hearts" are rightly confessed to our pastor. What is it about private confession that brings great comfort to troubled hearts?

3. In private confession with a pastor, what can Christians depend on:
   The pastor must
   The pastor must *not*

4. We plead guilty. Our Father declares us "not guilty" for the sake of His Son. In what ways does Christ's forgiveness help us to confess our sins openly to our heavenly Father? to our pastor or Christian brother or sister?

5. Because of Christ, what change does God's Spirit work in our hearts toward those who sin against us?

PRAYER
Heavenly Father, I admit and deplore my sinfulness, yet I rejoice that Your love in Christ brings me forgiveness and life. Help me not to judge others but to humbly carry out my vocation as Your servant for Jesus' sake. In His name I pray. Amen.

Church Keys

OFFICE OF THE KEYS

What is the Office of the Keys?
The Office of the Keys is that special authority which Christ has given to His church on earth to forgive the sins of repentant sinners, but to withhold forgiveness from the unrepentant as long as they do not repent.

> **Again Jesus said, "Peace be with you! As the Father has sent Me, I am sending you." And with that He breathed on them and said, "Receive the Holy Spirit. If you forgive anyone his sins, they are forgiven; if you do not forgive them, they are not forgiven. (John 20:21–23)**

FOR SHARING

1. Have you ever been locked out of your house or vehicle? Share the frustration you felt and your relief after you were able to get back in.

2. The Office of the Keys is a spiritual authority given by Christ to the church. What does this authority unlock? What does it lock?

3. Under what circumstances would a Christian withhold God's gift of forgiveness from another person?

4. The heart of the Gospel is that God has forgiven all sins for all people in the death of Christ. But before the human heart is ready to receive forgiveness, it must first recognize its sinfulness. How can we help people to recognize their sinfulness by the power of the Holy Spirit?

5. How can you "unlock" heaven for a family member, friend, or acquaintance?

PRAYER Heavenly Father, You have given to Your church the sacred responsibility of sharing Your Word of judgment and grace. Thank You for the gift of forgiveness and salvation in Christ. Use me to take Your message of life and peace to others so that they may know Your joy too. In Jesus' name. Amen.

OFFICE OF THE KEYS

What do you believe according to these words?
I believe that when the called ministers of Christ deal with us by His divine command, in particular when they exclude openly unrepentant sinners from the Christian congregation and absolve those who repent of their sins and want to do better, this is just as valid and certain, even in heaven, as if Christ our dear Lord dealt with us Himself.

> **"I will give you the keys of the kingdom of heaven; whatever you bind on earth will be bound in heaven, and whatever you loose on earth will be loosed in heaven." (Matthew 16:19)**

> **"I tell you the truth, whatever you bind on earth will be bound in heaven, and whatever you loose on earth will be loosed in heaven." (Matthew 18:18)**

FOR SHARING

1. An atheist once remarked, "What I envy most about you Christians is your forgiveness. I have nobody to forgive me."
   Describe, in your own words, life without forgiveness.

2. The pastor, as a "called and ordained servant of the Word," speaks for Christ on behalf of the entire congregation. How does receiving absolution from a pastor compare to receiving a pardon from the governor?

3. God's mercy is available to all people, but only those who are repentant and who trust in Christ receive forgiveness. What is true repentance? What is saving faith?

4. God's gift of forgiveness in Christ is free, but it isn't cheap. Explain.

5. Why does confession and absolution most often occur at the beginning of the Christian worship service?

PRAYER Heavenly Father, I come to You fully aware of my sinfulness. But I also know that I have been forgiven by Your Son's sacrifice on the cross. Give me wisdom and strength to point others to Your mercy in Jesus. Help me live in forgiveness with my brothers and sisters in Christ and with all people. In Jesus' name. Amen.

Royal Priesthood

PRIESTHOOD OF ALL BELIEVERS

Martin Luther once said, "It would please me very much if this word 'priest' were used as commonly as the term 'Christians' is applied to us. For it must be our aim to restore the little word 'priest' to the common use which the little word 'Christian' enjoys. ... When St. Peter says here: 'You are a royal priesthood,' this is tantamount to saying, 'You are Christians' " (LW, 30, pp. 63–64).

You are a chosen people, a royal priesthood, a holy nation, a people belonging to God, that you may declare the praises of Him who called you out of darkness into His wonderful light. (1 Peter 2:9)

FOR SHARING

1. "Membership has its privileges." What privileges have you received from membership in a community or neighborhood association?

2. In the Old Testament, the priest's "office" was to serve God in the sanctuary, God's house. A priest offered sacrifices to God on the people's behalf. What specific tasks does the pastor perform on behalf of the members of the congregation he is called to serve?

3. What is the distinction between the priesthood of all believers and the office of the public ministry?

4. Jesus is our "Great High Priest" whose sacrifice on the cross opens heaven to all believers. How did Jesus' sacrifice differ from those of the Old Testament priests?

5. To minister is to serve. In what sense is every Christian a minister?

PRAYER Heavenly Father, thank You for making me Your child through Holy Baptism. In Christ, You have called me to the priesthood of all believers. You have given me Your rich blessing to fulfill my calling. By the power of Your Holy Spirit, help me to represent You to everyone I meet. In Jesus' name I pray. Amen.

God's Gift in Pastors

OFFICE OF PUBLIC MINISTRY

"There are two ways of sending [the message of Christ]. First God sent His messengers, the prophets and apostles, like Moses and St. Paul, directly and without the help of an intermediary ... The other way of sending is indeed also one by God, but it is done through the instrumentality of man. It has been employed ever since God established the ministry with its preaching and exercise of the Office of the Keys. This ministry will endure and is not be replaced by any other. ... The ministry, that is, the Word of God, Baptism, and Holy Communion, came directly from Christ; but later Christ departed from this earth. Now a new way of sending was instituted, which works through man but is not of man ... according to it, we elect and send others, and we install them in their ministry to preach and administer the Sacraments. This type of sending is also of God and commanded by God (LW, 22, p. 482).

It was he who gave some to be apostles, some to be prophets, some to be evangelists, and some to be pastors and teachers, to prepare God's people for works of service, so that the body of Christ may be built up until we all reach unity in the faith and in the knowledge of the Son of God and become mature, attaining to the whole measure of the fullness of Christ. (Ephesians 4:11–13)

FOR SHARING

1. What are the typical expectations of pastors in today's world? How have the expectations changed over the years?

2. In what ways do pastors continue the apostles' preaching and teaching ministry?

3. "Our churches teach that nobody should preach publicly in the church or administer the sacraments unless he is regularly called" (Augsburg Confession XIV). Explain the benefits this teaching provides to the church.

4. The Lord who gave His life for the sins of the world also gives pastors to preach and teach the Gospel of forgiveness, life, and salvation. Give an example of a situation in which God brought a special blessing to His people through a pastor's ministry.

5. St. Paul wrote, "Respect those who work hard among you, who are over you in the Lord and who admonish you. Hold them in the highest regard in love because of their work" (1 Thessalonians 5:12–13). In what specific says can you *respect* and *regard* your pastor for his ministry in your congregation?

PRAYER Heavenly Father, thank You for pastors whom You have called to serve in the office of the public ministry. Bless them with Your forgiveness and strength. Send Your Holy Spirit on them so that they remain faithful to You and Your Word. Help me to treat them as Your messengers, called to serve in Jesus' name. Amen.

A Sacred Meal

THE SACRAMENT OF THE ALTAR

What is the Sacrament of the Altar?
It is the true body and blood of our Lord Jesus Christ under the bread and wine, instituted by Christ Himself for us Christians to eat and to drink.
The Holy Evangelists Matthew, Mark, Luke, and St. Paul write:

> Our Lord Jesus Christ, on the night when He was betrayed, took bread, and when He had given thanks, He broke it and gave it to the disciples and said: "Take, eat: this is My body, which given for you. This do in remembrance of Me."

> In the same way also He took the cup after supper, and when He had given thanks, He gave it to them, saying, "Drink of it, all of you; this cup is the new testament, in My blood, which is shed for you for the forgiveness of sins. This do, as often as you drink it, in remembrance of Me."

FOR SHARING

1. An English proverb notes, "Spread the table and contention will cease." Explain.

2. The Sacrament of the Altar is also known by other names. What does each name reveal about this sacred meal?
   Lord's Supper _____
   Lord's Table _____
   Holy Communion _____
   Breaking of the Bread _____
   Eucharist _____

3. Jesus is the Savior whose body and blood were given and shed on the cross for our forgiveness. Why did He give us the Sacrament of the Altar?

4. "This do in remembrance of Me." How does the Sacrament of the Altar recall Christ's sacrificial act for us and for our salvation?

5. Why do God's people most often receive the Sacrament together with other members of the body of Christ?

PRAYER

Lord Jesus, thank You for Your sacrifice on the cross. Baptized into Your name, I am Your forgiven child. I praise You for Your holy meal—Your body and blood given to me in, with, and under the bread and wine. Keep me close to You, and bring me often to Your table for the forgiveness, strength, and assurance You offer me there. In Jesus' name. Amen.

The Blessings of the Supper

THE SACRAMENT OF THE ALTAR

What is the benefit of this eating and drinking?
These words, "Given and shed for you for the forgiveness of sins," show us that in the Sacrament forgiveness of sins, life, and salvation are given us through these words. For where there is forgiveness of sins, there is also life and salvation.

> **The cup of blessing which we bless, is it not the communion of the blood of Christ? The bread which we break, is it not the communion of the body of Christ? For we, though many, are one bread and one body; for we all partake of that one bread. (1 Corinthians 10:16–17 NKJV)**

FOR SHARING

1. Alfred Hitchcock, who enjoyed food, was disappointed by the small portions at a dinner party he attended. As he prepared to leave, the hostess said, "I do hope you will dine with us again soon."
"By all means," Hitchcock replied. "Let's start now."
Besides actual food consumption, what are the benefits of eating in the company of others?

2. What reasons do Christians give for not regularly attending the Lord's Supper?

3. Luther writes, "We must never regard the Sacrament as a harmful thing from which we should flee, but as a pure, wholesome, soothing medicine which aids and quickens us in both soul and body. For where the soul is healed, the body has benefited also" (Large Catechism, V 68). Describe how the Lord's Supper is medicine for soul *and* body.

4. The forgiveness, life, and salvation given in the Lord's Supper are the blessings Christ earned for us at Calvary. How is the Lord's Supper unique among the ways God's people regularly receive these benefits?

5. In what way does the Lord's Supper connect us with Christ? with other believers, including the saints in heaven?

PRAYER Lord Jesus, every day I need Your forgiveness. Thank You for Your gift of forgiveness, life, and salvation You have earned for me at Calvary. Continue to draw me closer to You through Your body and blood in the Sacrament of the Altar. In Your name I pray. Amen.

THE SACRAMENT OF THE ALTAR

How can bodily eating and drinking do such great things?
Certainly not just eating and drinking do these things, but the words written here: "Given and shed for you for the forgiveness of sins." These words, along with the bodily eating and drinking, are the main thing in the Sacrament. Whoever believes these words has exactly what they say: "forgiveness of sins."

> **For I do not want you to be ignorant of the fact, brothers, that our forefathers were all under the cloud and that they all passed through the sea. They were all baptized into Moses in the cloud and in the sea. They all ate the same spiritual food and drank the same spiritual drink; for they drank from the spiritual rock that accompanied them, and that rock was Christ. (1 Corinthians 10:1–4)**

FOR SHARING

1. As a sign of affection Cleopatra is said to have once offered a guest a goblet of rich wine into which she had dissolved a pearl of great value. What priceless gifts do Christians receive together with bread and wine?

2. What makes the Lord's Supper a sacrament, rather than the mere consumption of bread and wine?

3. The host for this holy meal is the Lord Jesus. Why do you suppose St. Paul calls Him our "rock" in 1 Corinthians 10:3–4?

4. Bread and wine alone do not give forgiveness and faith, Luther notes, but "that bread and wine which are Christ's body and blood and with which the words are coupled. These and no other, we say, are the treasure through which forgiveness is obtained" (Large Catechism, V 28). Explain.

5. Tell what it means to you that Jesus has forgiven your sins.

PRAYER Good and gracious God, thank You for all the blessings that You give in the Lord's Supper. Help me to always remember that it is *Your* meal. Thank You for the forgiveness of all my sins through Your Sacrament. In Jesus' name I pray. Amen.

Worthy to Eat and Drink

THE SACRAMENT OF THE ALTAR

Who receives this sacrament worthily?
Fasting and bodily preparation are certainly fine outward training. But that person is truly worthy and well prepared who has faith in these words: "Given and shed for you for the forgiveness of sins." But anyone who does not believe these words or doubts them is unworthy and unprepared, for the words "for you" require all hearts to believe.

> **Whoever eats the bread or drinks the cup of the Lord in an unworthy manner will be guilty of sinning against the body and blood of the Lord. A man ought to examine himself before he eats of the bread and drinks of the cup. For anyone who eats and drinks without recognizing the body of the Lord eats and drinks judgment on himself. (1 Corinthians 11:27–29)**

FOR SHARING

1. A woman nervously approached her pastor before the service. "I can't take communion, Pastor. My faith is so weak. I'm not worthy."
   What would you say to her?

2. What is required of all who receive the Lord Supper?

3. Complete the following sentences: "As we examine ourselves, we ask whether we are _____ for our sins. We _____ in our Savior Jesus Christ and in His words in the Sacrament. We _____, with the help of the Holy Spirit, to change our sinful lives."

4. When is private confession with the pastor especially helpful in preparation to receiving the Lord's Supper?

5. Tell of a time when you most desired to receive the Lord's Supper

PRAYER

Merciful Lord, I am not worthy of Your love and forgiveness. I have sinned. At times my faith is weak. But I know I belong to You and You forgive me. Strengthen me, and help me to find a new beginning in You. In Jesus' name I pray. Amen.

Governments and Citizens

TABLE OF DUTIES: *OF CIVIL GOVERNMENT AND OF CITIZENS*

Certain passages of Scripture for various holy orders and positions, admonishing them about their duties and responsibilities.

Everyone must submit himself to the governing authorities, for there is no authority except that which God has established. The authorities that exist have been established by God. Consequently, he who rebels against the authority is rebelling against what God has instituted, and those who do so will bring judgment on themselves. (Romans 13:1–2)

Submit yourselves for the Lord's sake to every authority instituted among men: whether to the king, as the supreme authority, or to governors, who are sent by Him to punish those who do wrong and to commend those who do right. (1 Peter 2:13–14)

FOR SHARING

1. What is the general attitude toward government today? How, on the whole, do people view citizenship?

2. Do most people view authority as *mandated from above or supported from below?* Explain.

3. Summarize St. Paul and St. Peter's words on government and citizenship.

4. Jesus suffered punishment and death for our disobedience to God's Word and ways. What does Jesus' substitutionary work on your behalf mean to you?

5. God is a God of order and peace (1 Corinthians 14:33). How can we, as His redeemed people in Christ, contribute to order and peace in our congregations? our communities?

PRAYER

Heavenly Father, thank You for the blessings of government and citizenship in my life. In Christ, You have forgiven my failures to respect and honor Your authorities in the world. Help me to live as Your child and to accept the authorities You have placed in my life. By the power of Your Spirit enable me to be Your instrument of order and peace in the world around me. In Jesus' name. Amen.

Family Relations

TABLE OF DUTIES: *To Fathers and To Children*

Fathers, do not exasperate your children; instead, bring them up in the training and instruction of the Lord. (Ephesians 6:4)

Children, obey your parents in the Lord, for this is right. "Honor your father and mother"—which is the first commandment with a promise—"that it may go well with you and that you may enjoy long life on the earth." (Ephesians 6:1–3)

FOR SHARING

1. Share, as time permits, a joy you have experienced as a parent or child.

2. Where do you find your greatest challenge in bringing up your children "in the training and instruction of the Lord"?

3. In what ways do parents sometimes "exasperate" their children?

4. Share about a significant adult Christian role model in your life.

5. What changes would you like to make to facilitate spiritual growth in your family?

PRAYER Heavenly Father, help us to remember Your investment in our lives and keep us mindful of Your presence in our families. In Jesus' name. Amen.

The Solid Rock

CHRISTIAN QUESTIONS

5. *Do you hope to be saved?* Yes, that is my hope.
6. *In whom then do you trust?* In my dear Lord Jesus Christ.
7. *Who is Christ?* The Son of God, true God and man.
8. *How many Gods are there?* Only one, but there are three persons: Father, Son, and Holy Spirit?
9. *What has Christ done for you that you trust in Him?* He died for me and shed His blood for me on the cross for the forgiveness of sins.

> **But whatever was to my profit I now consider loss for the sake of Christ. What is more, I consider everything a loss compared to the surpassing greatness of knowing Christ Jesus my Lord, for whose sake I have lost all things. I consider them rubbish, that I may gain Christ and be found in Him, not having a righteousness of my own that comes from the law, but that which is through faith in Christ—the righteousness that comes from God and is by faith. (Philippians 3:7–9)**

FOR SHARING

1. "If you want a thing done well, do it yourself" (Napoleon I). What application of this perspective do you see in your life or in the lives of those around you?

2. In what ways do we show—by words and actions—our desire to be self-sufficient before God?

3. What does it mean to *trust in Jesus as Lord and Savior?*

4. Comment on Paul's words in Philippians 3:7–9. What do you consider "rubbish" in your life, that you may gain Christ and be found in Him?

5. In what respect is it difficult to trust solely in Christ for salvation? In what respect is this trust difficult?

PRAYER

My hope is built on nothing less Than Jesus' blood and righteousness;
No merit of my own I claim But wholly lean on Jesus' name.
On Christ, the solid rock, I stand; All other ground is sinking sand.

CHRISTIAN QUESTIONS

15. *What should we do when we eat His body and drink His blood, and in this way receive His pledge?* We should remember and proclaim His death and the shedding of His blood, as He taught us: This do, as often as you drink it, in remembrance of Me.

16. *Why should we remember and proclaim His death?* First, so we may learn to believe that no creature could make satisfaction for our sins. Only Christ, true God and man, could do that. Second, so we may learn to be horrified by our sins, and to regard them as very serious. Third, so we may find joy and comfort in Christ alone, and through faith in Him be saved.

17. *What motivated Christ to die and make full payment for your sins?* His great love for His Father and for me and other sinners, as it is written in John 14; Romans 5; Galatians 2 and Ephesians 5.

    You see, at just the right time, when we were still powerless, Christ died for the ungodly. Very rarely will anyone die for a righteous man, though for a good man someone might possibly dare to die. But God demonstrates His own love for us in this: While we were still sinners, Christ died for us. (Romans 5:6–8)

FOR SHARING

1. "From the cradle to the grave a man never does a single thing which has any first and foremost object but one—to secure peace of mind for himself" (Mark Twain). Agree or disagree. Explain your answer.

2. What was Jesus' motivation to go to the cross?

3. As the Holy Spirit works in the lives of God's people, how do we come to regard sin in our lives?

4. One aspect of participating in the Sacrament of the Altar involves remembering. Explain.

5. What does it mean to you to be saved by grace through faith in Jesus?

PRAYER

Love divine, all love excelling, Joy of heav'n, to earth come down!
Fix in us Thy humble dwelling, All Thy faithful mercies crown.
Jesus, Thou are all compassion, Pure, unbounded love Thou art;
Visit us with Thy salvation, Enter ev'ry trembling heart.